1940 EDITION

INDIAN

MILITARY MOTORCYCLE
Model 340

MANUAL OF CARE AND MAINTENANCE

U.S. ARMY TECHNICAL MANUAL TM-10-1283

INDIAN MOTOCYCLE COMPANY
SPRINGFIELD, MASSACHUSETTS   U.S.A.

©2013 Periscope Film LLC
All Rights Reserved
ISBN #978-1-940453-15-6

TM 10-1283

WAR DEPARTMENT,
Washington, October 13, 1941.

TM 10-1283, Maintenance Manual, Motorcycle, (Model 340 & 340B) published by Indian Motocycle Company, is furnished for the information and guidance of all concerned.

(AG 062.11 (4/26/41) PC (C), June 10, 1941.)

By order of the Secretary of War:

G. C. MARSHALL,
Chief of Staff.

Official:
   E. S. ADAMS,
      Major General,
         The Adjutant General.

FOREWORD

This book contains information necessary to the proper care and maintenance of the 1940 Indian 74 Military model motorcycle and sidecar.

Even though you are a good driver, we suggest that you familiarize yourself with the points mentioned in this care and maintenance manual.

In view of the fact that delivery of this equipment may be made to you in a partly disassembled condition, information is contained herein to enable you to properly assemble the handlebars, controls, sidecar, etc., to make the equipment ready for use.

This motorcycle has been designed and built to deliver a maximum of troublefree service. However, no amount of engineering ingenuity or care in the manufacture of this equipment can take the place of a reasonable amount of care and an avoidance of malpractices by the driver. A new machine requires more careful attention during the first "miles" of operation than at any other time in its life. To obtain best results, the motorcycle should not be driven at excessive speeds during these first "miles". A little extra care and attention given at this time will be fully repaid in longer service and more satisfactory performance. As the engine becomes "worked in" and operates more freely, full performance can then be expected.

Thru the proper care and maintenance as pointed out in this booklet, you can maintain the performance of your motorcycle at its highest peak of efficiency.

INDIAN MOTOCYCLE COMPANY

I N D E X

Battery	13
Brakes - adjustment of rear	11
Brakes - adjustment of front	11
Brakes - adjustment of sidecar	4
Brakes - relining	16
Brakes - control of	2
Carburetor	14
Chain, care of Rear Chain	10
Chain, care of Front Chain	11
Chain, adjustment of	10
Clutch, assembly pedal	2
Clutch, control of	6
Controls, Manipulation of	5
Controls, Assembly of	1
Distributor	12
Fork	16
Generator - care of	12
Generator - Belt	12
Handlebars	1
Headlight	12
Instruments	4
Lubrication chart	24
Motor - Starting	7
Motor - Lubrication of	6
Motor - Troubles & Remedies	20
Oil - Recommendations	8
Oil - Changing	9
Oiling System Tips	23
Saddle	13
Shifting	6
Sidecar - assembly of	3
Spark plugs	11
Spring Frame	17
Steering	14
Tanks	5
Transmission (Lubrication of)	8
Trouble Saving Tips	19
Valve Adjustment	13
Wheels, motorcycle	9
Wheels, sidecar	16
Wheels, care	10
Wheels, Bearing Replacement	16

****

ILLUSTRATIONS

Sidecar Chassis Connections.	3A
Wiring Diagram	4A
Instruments - Controls	4B
Oiling Pump Diagram	6A
Front Wheel.	9A
Rear Wheel	9B
Front Chain.	10A
Front Brake.	10B
Carburetor	14A
Spring Frame	17A
Lubrication	25A

ASSEMBLY INSTRUCTIONS FOR MOTORCYCLES
DELIVERED IN A PARTLY ASSEMBLED CONDITION

To Assemble The Handlebars and Controls

Remove the round headed handlebar nut, the flat washer and cover plate from the fork stem. Set the handlebars on the fork head. Take the three wires with eyes on end of wires (insulated with rubber tubing) and run them on the right side of the frame between the frame head and forkshield through the clip located on front top tank bolt, then to the instrument panel. With the instrument panel removed, looking at the switch from a riding position, attach the red wire with the red marker to the terminal marked in red on the switch. The speedometer light wire is also attached to this terminal.

The horn wire is black with a green tracer and attaches to the left side of the switch at the terminal marked in green.

The long wire in this group is the parking light wire. It is marked with a yellow tracer and attaches to the terminal on the switch marked in yellow.

Take the rubber tube that has the three black wires with no color markings and pass them thru the hole in the fork shield. These three wires are for the high, low and parking lights in the headlight. The wire from the switch is the parking light wire. Plug this wire into the center hole of the headlight terminal. Plug the other two wires in either hole.

The two wires leading thru the handlebar top attach to the horn.

TO CONNECT THE CONTROLS

The control cable operating from the right handlebar grip is for the "Spark" control. The control cable operating from the left handlebar grip is for the carburetor or "gas" control.

Take the "spark" control cable and pass it to the left of the frame (between the fork and frame head), then pass it thru the clip located on lower front tank bolt on the left side of the machine. Then pass it thru the clip located on top of the ignition coil (at base of front cylinder). Then pass it to the distributor control arm. Pass the wire end of the cable thru the lock provided at the distributor arm. Turn the right grip clockwise as far as it will go. At the distributor, pull the control arm out (away from the motor base) as far as it will go. This will be a fully retarded position. Then lock the control wire in position with the set screw provided at the control arm.

Turn the handlebar control grip to the right and left to make sure that a full retard and full advance setting is obtained. Then lock the cable in position at the coil clamp.

Take the "gas" control cable and pass it to the right of the frame (between the fork and frame head), then pass it thru the clamp located on the lower front tank bolt on the right side of the machine. Cross the cable over to the left side of the machine underneath the tank and thru the clip located on the left side of the front cylinder head. Then pass the wire end of the cable thru the adjustment provided at the carburetor control arm. Turn the left handlebar grip counterclockwise as far as it will go. Push carburetor control lever back (towards the rear cylinder) as far as it will go. Lock the control wire in position at the control arm. Now turn the handlebar grip to the left and right to make sure that you have a full throw of the carburetor control lever. Counterclockwise shuts the "gas" off - clockwise turns the "gas" on to a full open throttle.

Lock the control cable in position at the cylinder head clamp.

TO TIGHTEN THE HANDLEBARS

When all wires and controls are connected, press the handlebars down onto the fork stems as far as they will go. Put the cover plate over the fork stem. Place the flat washer on the center fork stem. Put on handlebar nut and tighten down. Turn flat washer "up" on side of nut to lock the nut in position.

Assemble horn brackets to the two bolts located thru the handlebars. Attach horn to these brackets and tighten all nuts and bolts. Attach horn wires.

FRONT BRAKE CONTROL

Attach front brake control lever to the right handlebar between the horn button and "spark" control grip.

ASSEMBLING THE CLUTCH PEDAL

Place the friction washer on the pedal shaft. Then place the metal washer on this same shaft. A 1/4" hole is drilled off center in this metal washer. This fits on the pin of the frame lug. Place the pedal shaft thru the hole in the frame lug. Assemble spring and castellated nut on the pedal shaft. Tighten this nut so that the spring will have just enough tension to hold the clutch pedal in a disengaged position with the clutch rod attached. Cotter pin the nut.

ASSEMBLING THE SIDECAR

Place the sidecar wheel on the wheel spindle. Bolt the wheel to the brake drum. (6 studs). Now take the fender. Loosen the two clamps on the front end of this fender. Slide the clamps and fender over the tubular brace extending outward in front of the sidecar wheel. Bring the fender down over the sidecar wheel. Attach the inside fender braces to the lugs on the chassis. Attach the outside braces to the wheel spindle, using the spacer on the spindle between the wheel and the braces. Bolt into place and tighten all connections.

CONNECTING THE SIDECAR TO THE MOTORCYCLE

On the right front of the motorcycle frame just underneath the right footboard, you will find a clevis connection. This is the front sidecar chassis connection. Remove the bolt in this clevis and swing the front of the sidecar chassis into place in this clevis. Slip the bolt thru the clevis to hold this connection in place.

At the rear wheel, near the rear axle, is another clevis connection. Remove the clevis bolt, noting the spacing washers.

Place the rear sidecar chassis connection into place and slide the bolt into position. Use the six spacing washers on both sides of this connection to locate the proper position.

Draw up both front and rear connections snugly and cotter pin the castellated nuts.

THE SIDECAR AND MOTORCYCLE BRACE CONNECTION

The third connection of the sidecar chassis to the motorcycle consists of a brace running from the rear of the sidecar chassis up to a connection bolt located just under the saddle of the motorcycle.

Attach the tube end of this brace underneath the sidecar body and springs to the rear cross member of the sidecar chassis. A special clamp type lug is provided to make this attachment. The brace should be attached in front of the sidecar cross member.

A second clamp is provided to attach this brace in a similar manner at a point on the sidecar cross member just inside the left spring. Leave both of these connections slightly loose.

Attach the "eye" end of this brace at the connection bolt under the saddle on the motorcycle.

You are now ready to align the sidecar to the motorcycle.

Make sure that tire pressures are correct. Front tire, 20 lbs. Rear motorcycle tire, 25 lbs. Sidecar tire, 20 lbs.

Attaching Sidecar to Motorcycle

Labels (from image):
- Front Connection Clamp
- Front Chassis Connection Clevis
- Sidecar Brake Rod Connection
- Rear Chassis Connection Clevis
- "Eye" end of Brace Connects under Saddle on Machine
- Sidecar Brace from Chassis to Motorcycle
- Rear Body Bolts
- Sidecar Chassis Cross Member
- Front Body Bolts
- Sidecar Brace Connections to Chassis Cross Member
- Fender Clips

3A

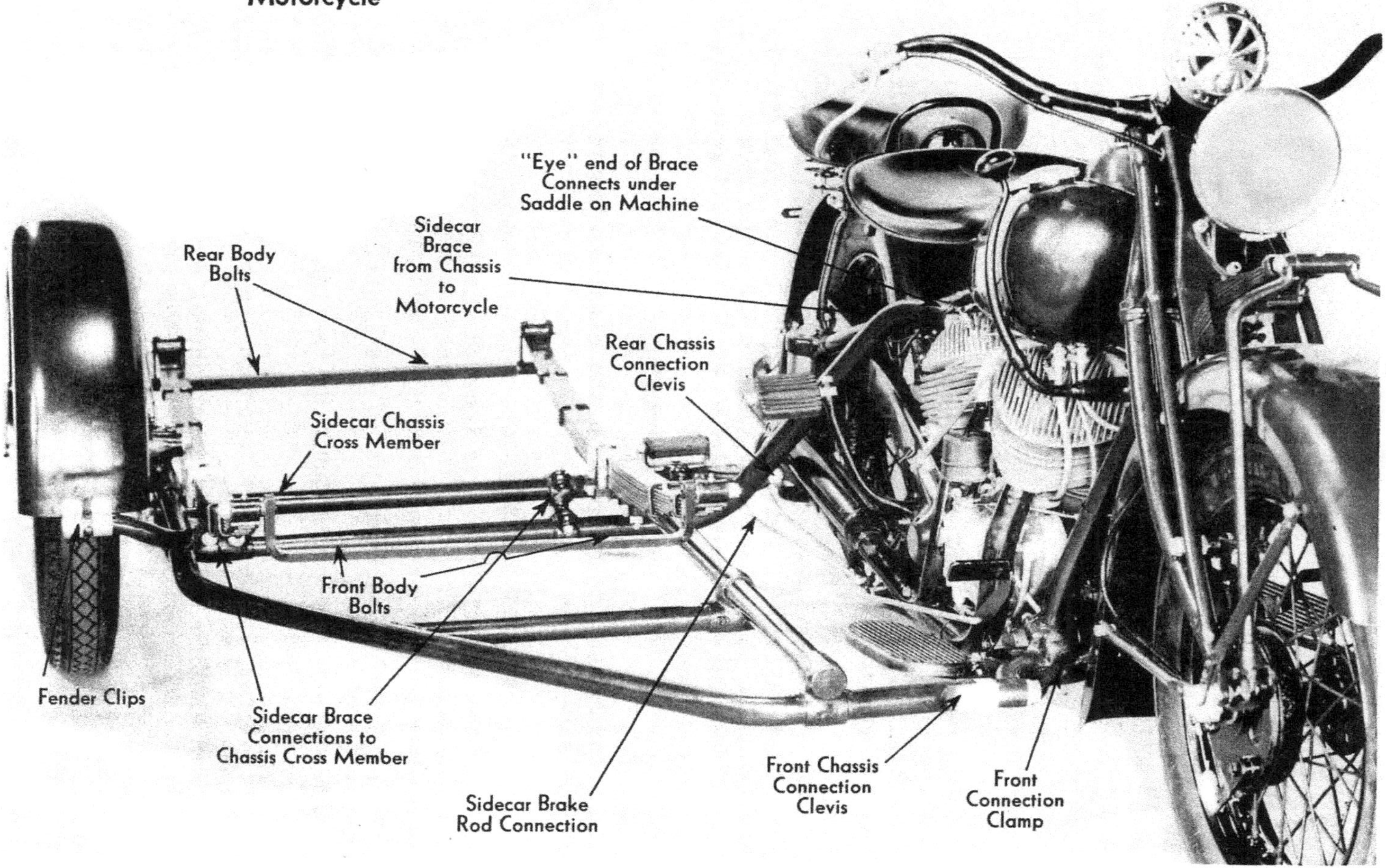

TO ALIGN THE SIDECAR

Making sure that the machine is resting on a fairly level floor, tilt the motorcycle away from the sidecar between two and three degrees (2° or 3°).

Then tighten all brace connections, cotter pinning all castellated nuts.

The machine when properly aligned should operate in a straight line without any side pull.

SIDECAR BRAKE CONNECTIONS

At a point on the rear of the motorcycle where the sidecar connection is made, you will note, a brake rod with clevis attachment. This attaches to the brake arm at the sidecar connection.

In order to secure a proper adjustment of this sidecar brake, a road test is necessary. When properly adjusted, there should not be any side pull whatever with the brake pedal firmly applied. If there is a side pull, adjust the brake rod clevis connection until the machine can be "braked" in a straight line.

INSTRUMENTS

All instruments are located in the panel on the front top side of the fuel tanks.

The left dial is the ammeter.

Just to the right of this is located the ignition and light control switch. The knob when turned counterclockwise (to the left) as far as it will go is in an "off" position.

One notch to the right turns on the ignition only.

Two notches to the right turns on the ignition and the headlight.

Three notches to the right turns on the parking light only.

The high and low headlight beam control switch is located on the left handlebar just in front of the gas control grip. This operates only when the ignition switch in the panel is turned to the second notch.

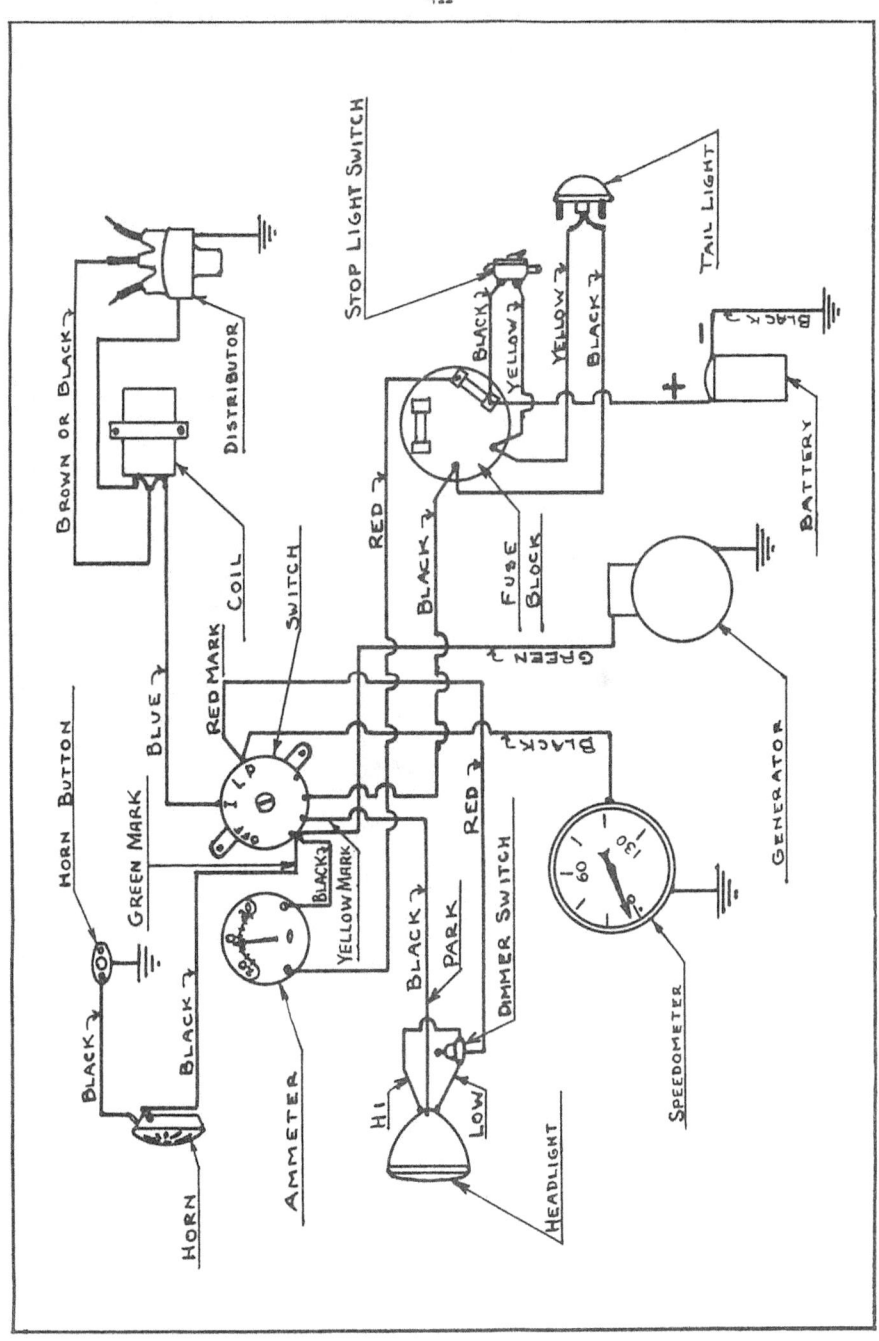

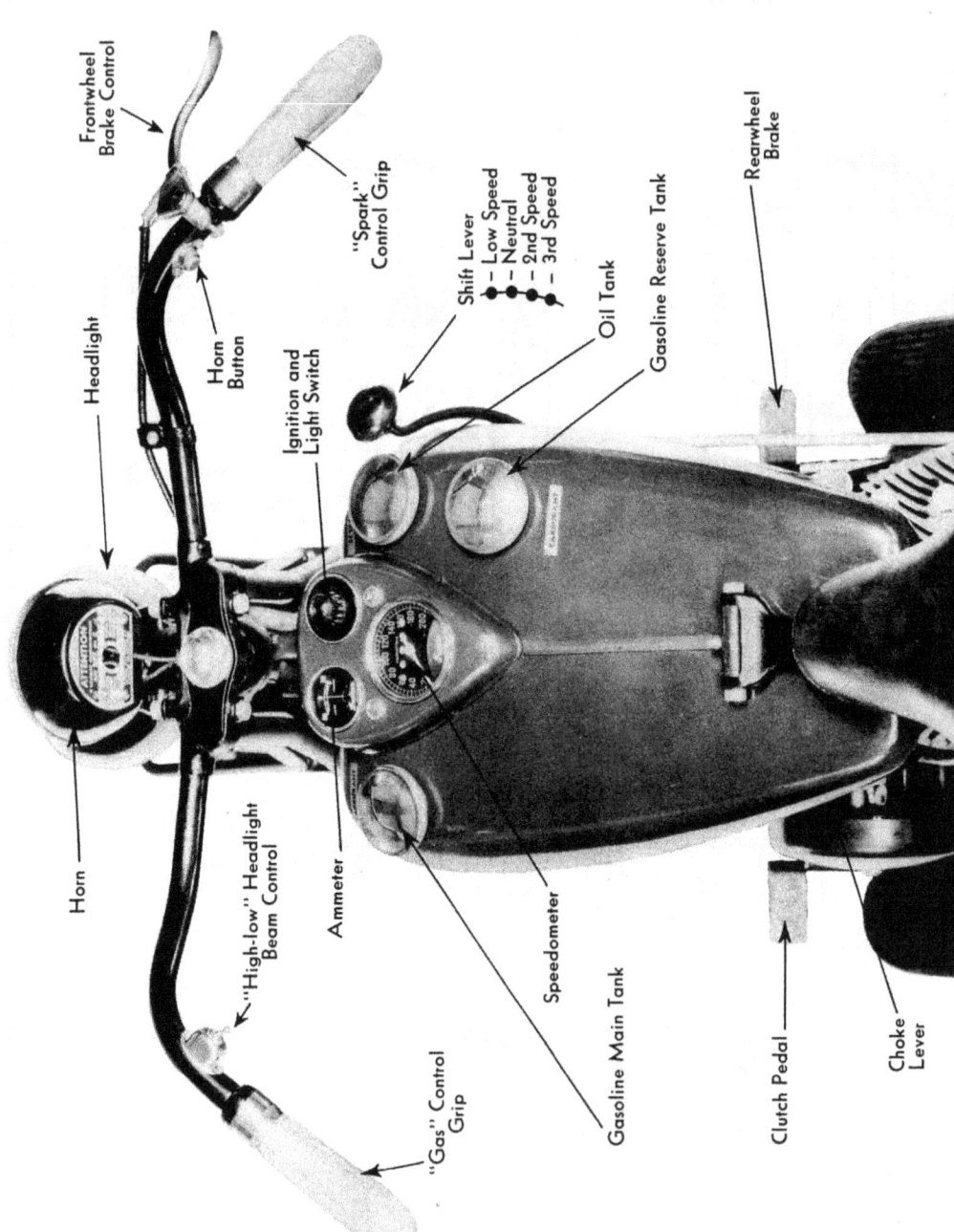

The large instrument in the instrument panel is the speedometer and is equipped with an indirect light which operates with the headlights for night driving. The speedometer is of the direct drive governor type and is extremely accurate to a very high speed range.

FILLING THE GASOLINE AND OIL TANKS

The fuel tanks on the motorcycle are made up in two separate halves. The left half being the main gasoline tank, having one filler cap; the right half housing two built-in compartments, one for a gasoline reserve supply and the other for the oil supply. The forward section of this right half is for oil storage and has a capacity of 2.3 quarts. The rear compartment (toward the driver) is for gasoline. The gasoline capacity of the main and reserve tanks together is 3.5 gallons. Separate tank shut-offs are provided underneath each tank.

The filler caps are of the bayonet type and require only a half turn to remove or lock into position.

To fill the gasoline tanks, remove the caps from the left tank and the right rear tank. Fill to within one inch of the top with gasoline.

Remove the filler cap from the front opening of the right tank.

If you will look into this opening, you will see a tube extending upward towards the opening. This is the oil return line from the engine. Fill this oil tank with Indian Oil to within 2" of the upper end of this return tube. (see lubrication chart on page 8 for the proper grade of oil). Replace filler cap and turn until locked. This oil tank is vented from underneath.

MANIPULATION OF CONTROLS

Throttle and Spark Controls

The spark advance and throttle are controlled by "twisting" grips. Turning the left grip inward (to the right) opens the throttle; turning it outward (to the left) closes the throttle. Turning the right grip inward (to the left) advances the spark; turning it outward (to the right) retards the spark. A simple rule to remember is: Turning both grips "inward" increases the speed and turning them outward decreases the speed.

Brake Controls

The front wheel brake is operated by applying pressure to the hand lever on the right handlebar. The brake releases when pressure ceases. The rear wheel brake is operated by a pedal on the right footboard. This brake holds only as long as the pedal is held down.

Clutch Control

The clutch is controlled by a rocker pedal at the left footboard. Pressing down the toe or forward pad disengages the clutch. Pressing down the heel or rear pad engages the clutch.

Shifting The Gears

The clutch must be disengaged before shifting gears. Neglect of this may cause breakage of some part of the driving mechanism or transmission. Disengagement must be complete in order to have a proper shift.

Motor Lubrication
(see illustration 6A)

The lubricating system is what is known as "dry sump lubrication" which means that the oil is pumped from the storage tank to the motor in sufficient quantity to automatically lubricate properly all parts of the motor at any speed, after which the surplus oil is returned to the tank by means of a return pump thru a filter unit and outside cooling lines.

SPECIAL ATTENTION MUST BE GIVEN
TO THE FOLLOWING:

1. Break the motor in properly.
2. Shift gears correctly at all times.
3. Use the correct spark plugs.
4. Watch your tappet adjustment.
5. Use the correct fuel. And above all, use the RIGHT oil.

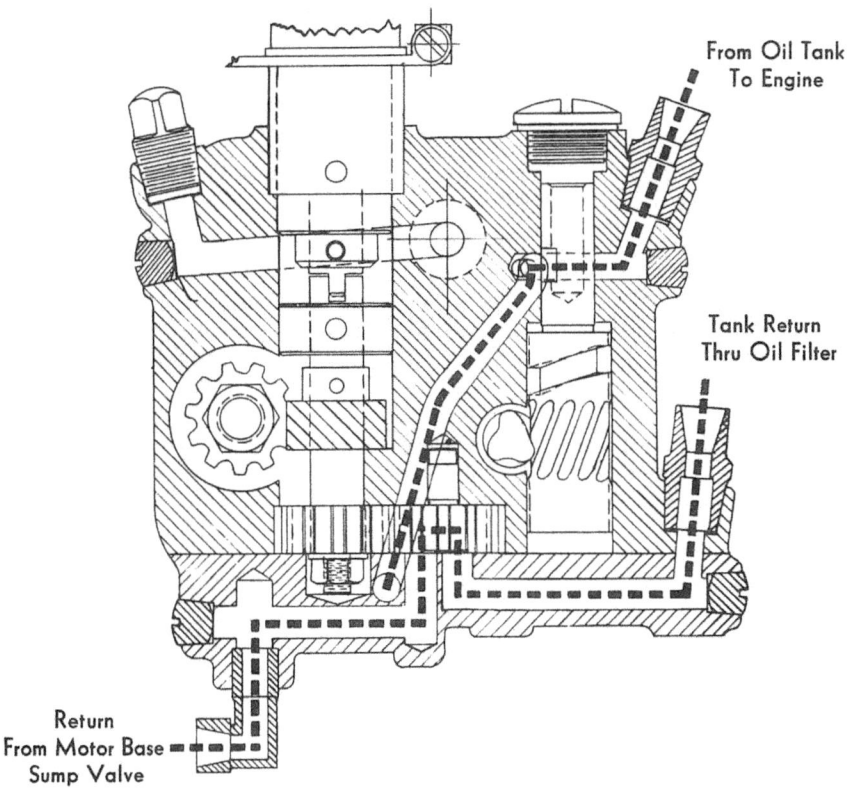

STARTING THE MOTOR

1. Open the gasoline tank shutoff located underneath the gasoline tank. Separate shutoffs are provided for each tank. To open, turn either one counterclockwise.

2. Set the gear shift lever in a "Neutral" position. The gear shift lever when pushed forward as far as it will go will be in "low" or first speed. Back towards the driver one (1) notch is "Neutral". Back towards the driver two (2) notches is "2nd" or intermediate speed. Back three (3) notches is "3rd" or high speed.

3. See that the clutch pedal is set in a fully engaged position. (With the heel plate of the clutch pedal pressed back towards the footboard as far as it will go, the clutch will be in a fully engaged position. Pressing down on the toe plate of the clutch pedal releases the clutch).

4. Check to make sure the ignition switch is in an "Off" position.

5. Prime the motor by turning the motor over two or three times with the kick starter. The kick starter is located directly underneath the saddle on the right side of the machine and is equipped with a rubber foot pedal to give the foot ample support to kick over the motor.

    (a) - First kick should be with the "gas" control handlebar grip (left one) wide open. (Clockwise as far as it will go gives a wide open throttle).

    The "Choke" lever, located behind the carburetor air cleaner should be in a down or choked position.

    (b) - Second kick should be made with a completely closed throttle (counterclockwise as far as it will go) and the "choke" lever one notch "up" from the previous choked position.

6. Now turn on the ignition switch. Twist the right grip "spark" control counterclockwise as far as it will go, then clockwise a fraction of a turn. This will put the "spark" control in a slightly retarded position from full advance.

7. Kick the motor over again with the kickstarter, with a good strong kick.

8. As soon as the motor starts, open the throttle just far enough to keep it running while warming up, or until ready to get under way. A cold motor should be allowed a few seconds to get partially warmed up. When the motor begins to warm up, move the choke lever up one more notch. This will be only one notch away from an open position. After the motor is completely warmed up, move the choke lever to "open" position "all the way UP" (towards the tank).

Starting a hot motor does not always require the use of the choke lever on the carburetor.

Racing a motor on the stand is the worst abuse that can be inflicted on it and should never be permitted at any time.

RECOMMENDED GRADES OF INDIAN OIL

Grade Names	S.A.E. No.	Navy Symbol No.
Indian Light	10W	2110
Indian Light Medium	20W	3050
Indian Medium	30	3065
Indian Heavy	50	1100

FOR ALL TEMPERATURES

1. Above 60° F. - Use SAE 50.
2. Between 60° F. and 32° F. - Use SAE 30.
3. Between 32° F. and 0° F. - Use SAE 20W.
4. Below 0° F. - Use SAE 10W.

The same grade of oil is used in the primary drive (clutch case) as is used in the motor.

If the clutch is inclined to drag when cold, use the next lighter grade of oil in the clutch case.

LUBRICATION OF THE CLUTCH AND TRANSMISSION

The old oil in the clutch and in the transmission should occasionally be drained and replaced with fresh oil. The oil level should be checked every 500 miles. If low, fill with fresh oil.

To change clutch oil, remove the drain plug from the bottom of the clutch case and allow all the oil to drain off. Replace the plug. The filler plug is located on top of the case. Remove this plug, also the oil level screw located just below the clutch operating arm on the face of the case. Pour enough Indian Oil in through the filler hole to bring the oil level to the lower edge of the level screw hole. Replace both level screw and filler cap. If the clutch is inclined to drag when the motor is cold, change to a lighter grade of oil.

To change the lubricant in the transmission, drain by removing the plug from the bottom of the transmission case. Refill through the filler hole located on the cover of the case. Pour enough transmission lubricant (600W) into the case to bring the oil level up to the lower edge of the level screw hole located also on the lower right side of the case. Replace both oil level screw and filler cap.

CHANGING TO FRESH OIL

The old oil should be drained from oil tank every 800 to 1000 miles by removing drain plug underneath the tank. Drain the crank case by removing the plug at the bottom of the crank case on the left side of the motor. Clean out oil tank by flushing with gasoline.

REMOVING THE WHEELS
(see illustration 9A)

The front, rear, and side car wheels are interchangeable. The brake drum always remains in place when the wheel is removed.

TO REMOVE THE FRONT WHEEL

To remove the front wheel, take off the axle nut (B) on the right side of the machine, loosen and remove the six taper head bolts (D) holding the wheel to the brake drum, and pull out the axle (C) from the left hand side. Pull the wheel to the left away from the brake drum assembly and free of the machine. When assembling, be sure all nuts are tightened.

TO REMOVE THE REAR WHEEL
(see illustration 9B)

To remove the rear wheel, remove the bolts that hold the left fender braces to the frame and take the braces off. Then remove the axle nut (D) on the right side of the machine, loosen and remove the six taper head bolts holding the wheel to the brake drum and pull out the axle from the left hand side. Pull

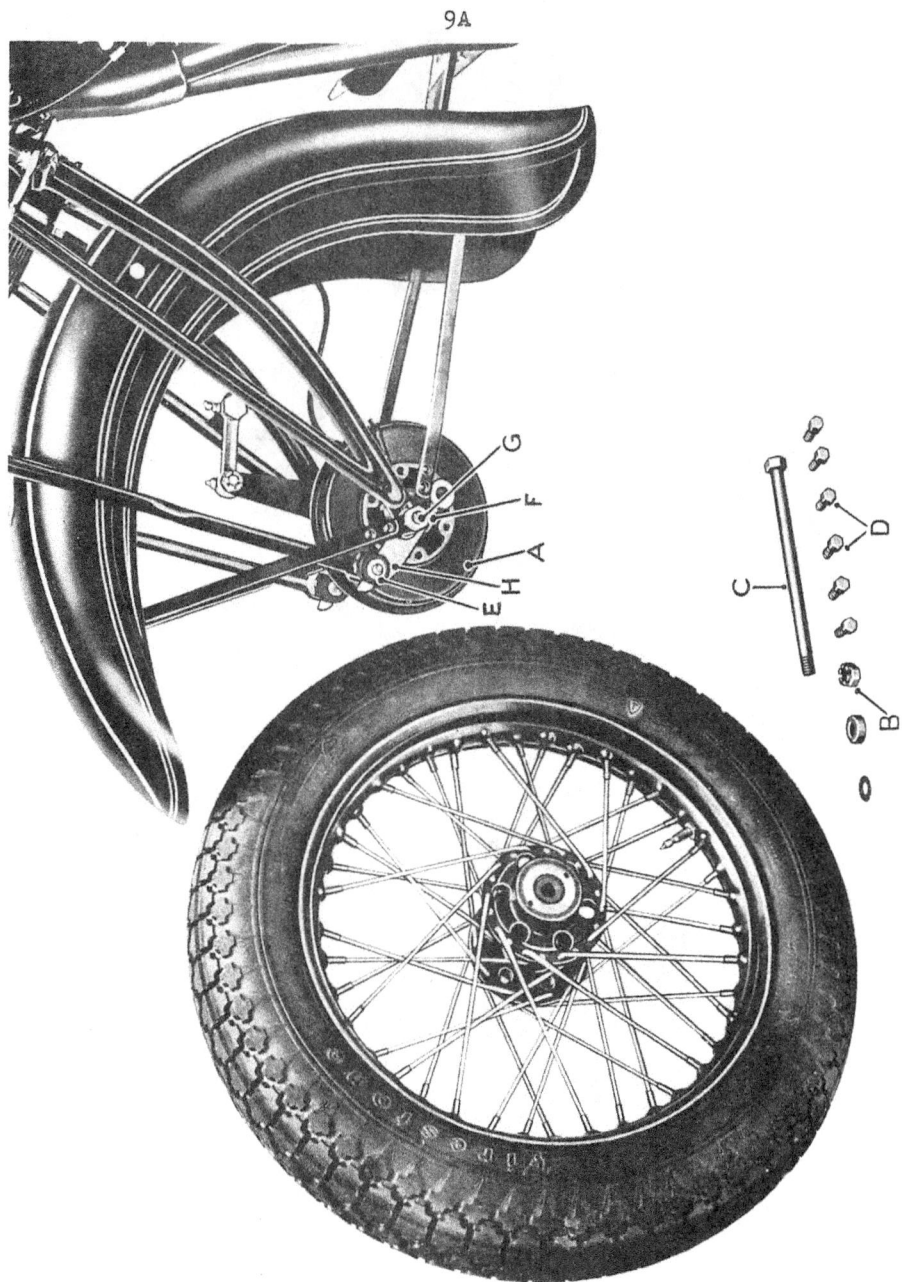

the wheel to the left away from the brake drum and free of the machine. When assembling, be sure all nuts are tightened. It is not necessary when removing the wheel only to take off the brake drums.

CARE OF WHEEL BEARINGS

Front and Rear Wheels

The bearings in all wheels are of a special design that automatically take care of thrust and therefore will need no adjustment. The bearing on the left side of the wheel should be greased every 500 miles while the right side bearing should be lightly greased with high temperature grease, such as Indian Wheel Bearing Grease, every 2500 miles. Care should be taken not to put too much grease in the brake drum wheel bearing. The lubricator fitting is in the rim of the brake drum.

CARE OF THE REAR CHAIN

Keep the chain at the proper tension at all times. This can be determined by lifting the bottom of the chain at its center. It should lift only about one inch if properly adjusted. A loose chain may jump the sprockets and damage spokes and chain guard. Tight chains cause extra wear on the bearings and result in chain breakage.

Occasionally, disconnect and remove the chain. Clean it with kerosene thoroughly, then wipe it dry and dip in a mixture of light cylinder oil and graphite. After an hour in the mixture, hang the chain up to dry. When all dripping ceases, wipe off excess mixture and oil and put the chain on its sprockets. Be sure that the clip of the detachable link snaps into proper position. The split, or open end of this spring clip should be pointing in the opposite direction to chain-travel.

TO ADJUST THE REAR CHAIN
(see illustration 9B)

Loosen the center axle nut (D) on the right hand side of the machine also nut (E) that holds the brake and sprocket assembly to the rear fork end. Tighten the adjusting screw (G) in each fork end an equal amount until the chain runs true on its sprockets, and there is no tight spot. The wheel should run squarely in the frame. Tighten both center (E) and hollow axle

10A

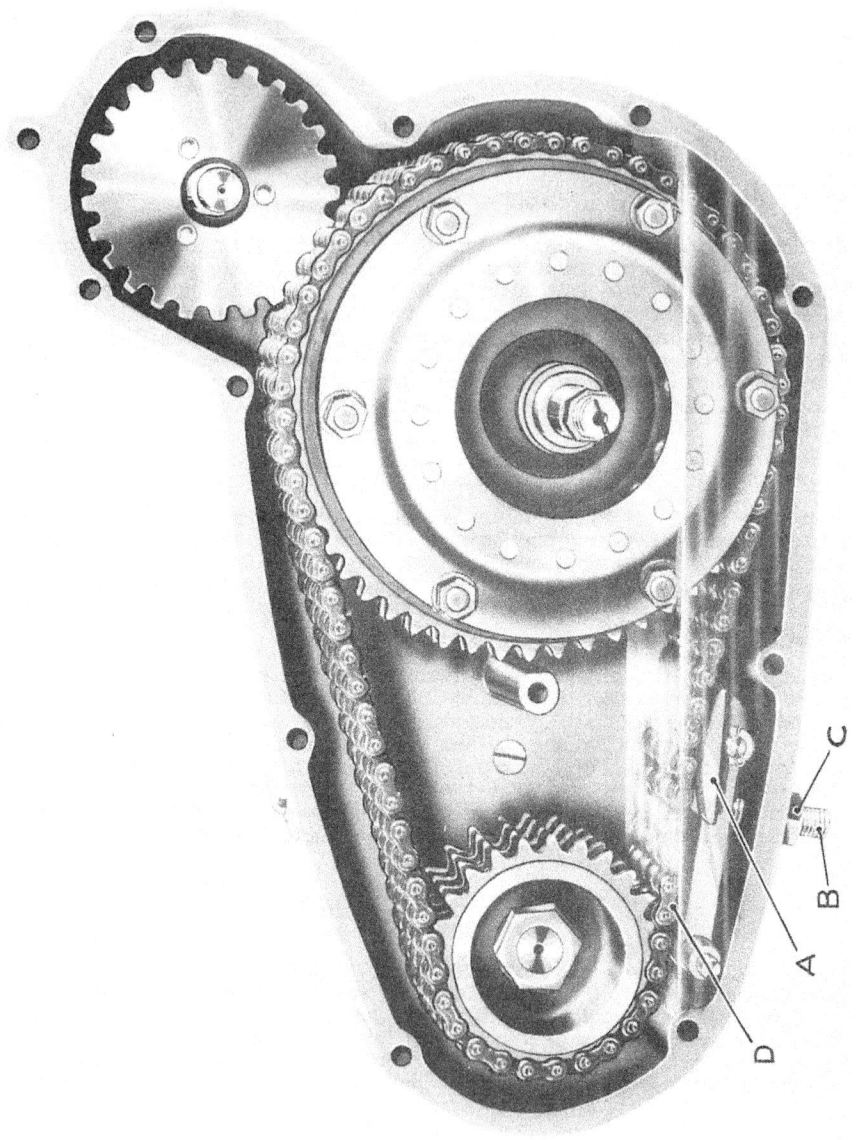

(D) nuts securely. Screw adjusting screws down tight against the lug on frame after the axle is tight in order to prevent them from backing out and lock with check nut (F). In taking up the chain, it will be necessary to check length of brake rod (C) to make up for the change in the wheel location.

TO ADJUST THE FRONT CHAIN
(see illustration 10A)

Excessive slack in the primary drive chain is taken up by means of a shoe (A) under the chain (D) which can be raised or lowered by means of a screw and lock nut (B & C) on the under side of the primary drive case, however DO NOT RUN THE CHAIN TIGHT. Remove the plug from the inspection hole located on the upper face of the cover and insert a small rod or tool under the chain, testing it for slack. When the chain can be moved freely up and down a distance equal to the diameter of the inspection hole, or approximately 3/4", it is properly adjusted.

ADJUSTING THE REAR WHEEL BRAKES
(see illustration 9B)

Adjustments for the rear wheel brake may be made by shortening the brake rod. Remove clevis pin (A), loosen lock nut (B) and turn clevis (C) to the right. TIGHTEN LOCK NUT (B) AFTER MAKING BRAKE ADJUSTMENT. Be sure to keep the rear wheel brake lever bearing well lubricated, alemite fitting provided on brake arm at brake drum.

ADJUSTING FRONT WHEEL BRAKE
(see illustration 10B)

Front wheel brake may be adjusted by changing the length of brake cable casing (A) at the cable anchorage on the brake drum plate. Loosen check nut (B) and screw sleeve nut (C) left or out to tighten brake. Further adjustment may be made by loosening cable nut (H) at the brake arm and pulling the wire cable through. Then tighten nut.

CARE OF SPARK PLUGS

Spark plugs should be kept clean and the points free from blisters. The correct spark gap is from .022" to .025".

CARE AND ADJUSTMENT OF GENERATOR

Add four or five drops of a good light machine oil every 500 miles to oilers on both ends of the generator.

The generator is of the third brush type. To increase the output, move the third, or adjustable brush, in the direction of the rotation of the armature. To decrease the output, move the third brush in the opposite direction from the rotation of the armature.

For generator output adjustment, fitted to your riding needs consult your service mechanic. Never set the charging rate too high, thus preventing the injurious overcharging of the battery.

CARE AND ADJUSTMENT OF DISTRIBUTOR

Distributor breaker points should be examined occasionally to be sure that they are clean and in proper adjustment. If they are dirty or pitted, polish them with a special breaker point file. Adjust to .020" gap when open.

The distributor cap should be kept clean and free of grease or dust. All wires should be clean and properly seated in cap sockets.

CONNECTING AND ADJUSTING HEAD LAMP

The head lamp is of the prefocus type and needs no bulb adjustment. The beam of lamp may be lowered or raised by loosening the anchor bolt and tilting the headlight to the proper angle. The switch on the left handlebar is the hi-lo beam control. Plug in the two wires from switch having plug-in terminals into the lamp. Attach the other switch wire, with loop terminal, to the proper terminal of instrument panel switch (see assembly instructions on page 1). Attach parking wire to center plug of headlamp and connect to proper terminal of switch (see wiring diagram on page 4A).

TO TIGHTEN GENERATOR BELT

If the generator belt becomes loose so that the generator pulley does not turn when the motor is running, loosen the two bolts that hold the generator to the generator bracket. Move the generator away from the driving pulley until the belt will not slip over the pulleys when tried by hand. Tighten the bracket bolts.

CARE OF BATTERY

The battery of this motorcycle is of the latest Indian design and is equipped with both "outside filler caps" and "fill-rite" safety vents.

To fill the battery to the proper level -- remove the filler caps for each cell. Press down on the rubber button for the cell being filled and add distilled water until it overflows. Upon removing your finger from the rubber button, the water level of the cell just filled will drop to the correct level. Repeat for each cell.

Keep the battery properly filled with distilled water and the terminals coated with vaseline to prevent corrosion. The battery hold-down screw should be tightened only enough to keep the battery from shifting.

Make a habit of checking the battery regularly for water and gravity of solution.

ADJUSTING THE VALVE TAPPETS

The proper running of motor depends in a large measure upon the good condition of the valves. All valves have adjustable tappets to compensate for wear. The intake valves are those nearest the carburetor in each cylinder, while the exhaust valves are those farthest away from the carburetor.

It is important to have the clearance or distance between the tappet and the end of the valve stem correct, if the motor is to run quietly and keep its power and speed. The proper clearance for the intake valve is five thousandths (.005) of an inch. The proper clearance for the exhaust valve is seven-thousandths (.007) of an inch. If motor is intended to be run at high speed the clearance should be .006 on inlet tappets and .008 on exhaust tappets. **MAKE ALL TAPPET ADJUSTMENTS WITH A COLD MOTOR.**

SADDLE ADJUSTMENTS

All saddle springs are designed at the factory for maximum riding comfort. The seat post springs may be changed by removing the nut and washer underneath the motorcycle and lifting the seat post assembly out of the frame from the top.

To increase the seat post spring tension - loosen check nut and screw collar at base of springs - up. This compresses the springs creating greater tension. Tighten lock nut.

Provisions are made for moving the saddle backward and forward by two holes provided in the saddle bracket, and a long slot in the saddle front connection. To adjust, loosen the nuts, holding the nose of the saddle to the front connection, and remove the seat post and bracket bolt. Move the saddle to the desired position and replace the bolt, tightening all nuts.

When properly adjusted, the seat post link should be in a vertical position.

ADJUSTING STEERING HEAD BEARING

To check the adjustment of the steering head bearing, jack up the front end of the motorcycle so that the front wheel is clear, then turn the handlebars to the right and left. There should be a very slight drag if the bearing is properly adjusted. If there is no drag, or too much drag, loosen the two bolts, take off the handlebars, remove the flat washer which is bent over the edge of the adjusting cone, then adjust the steering head bearing just enough so that there is a slight drag. It will be necessary before replacing the large flat washer to flatten the bent portion and then bend it down over the adjusting cone in proper position. When the adjustment is satisfactory, the handlebars should be put in place, and large hexagonal nut on the top tightened down securely. Then the two bolts may be tightened to hold the handlebars firmly against the fork sides (see assembling instructions on page 1).

ADJUSTING THE CARBURETOR
(see illustration 14A)

The carburetor is equipped with two adjustable needle valves, one for high speed adjustment and one for low speed adjustment so that an extremely accurate adjustment for any climatic condition may be easily accomplished.

If the carburetor has not previously been adjusted to the motor or if for any reason it is out of adjustment, proceed as follows:

Turn both needle valves (4 & 3) to the right (clockwise) until they seat (care being taken not to use force which might result in injuring the seat). Turn high speed needle (No. 4) (needle nearest front of machine) to left (counterclockwise) two (2) full turns. Turn the low speed needle (No. 3) (rear needle valve) in the same direction two (2) full turns.

14A

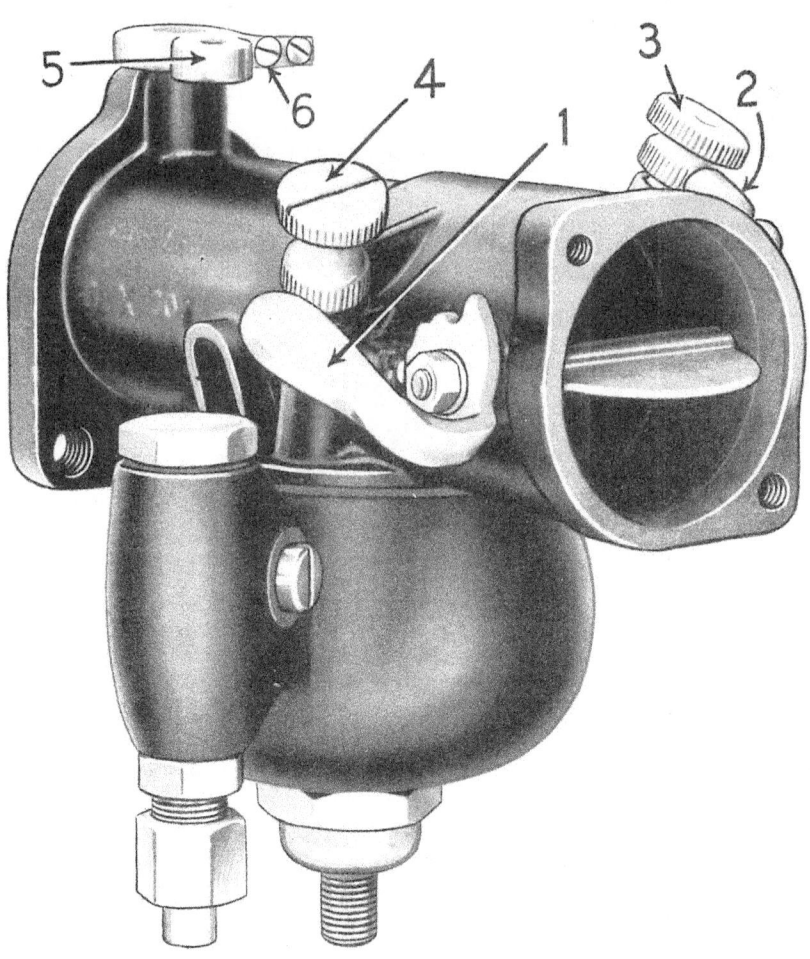

Start the motor and allow it to run until warm. Then with the spark retarded halfway and the choke lever open, adjust the rear needle valve (low speed No. 3) until the motor fires evenly. (Turning the needle valve to the right (clockwise) gives a leaner mixture and turning it to the left (counterclockwise) gives a richer mixture).

When a proper idling mixture is obtained the speed of the motor should be regulated by means of adjusting the rear screw (No. 6) on throttle lever at the carburetor.

To get the proper high speed adjustment, have the spark retarded half-way and open the throttle for a fraction of a second. If the motor backfires through the carburetor, it indicates that the mixture is too lean. The front needle valve (No. 4) should be turned to the left (counterclockwise) about 1/2 turn. If the motor chokes when the throttle is opened, it indicates that the mixture is too rich and needle valve (No. 4) should be turned to the right (clockwise) about 1/2 turn. Repeat this operation until a satisfactory mixture has been obtained.

Although the high and low needle valves operate independently, they nevertheless influence each other to a certain extent and it is therefore necessary that the entire carburetor adjustment instructions given above be repeated several times before a satisfactory adjustment is obtained.

It should be borne in mind that the carburetor will perform with a rich mixture but this is wasteful. On the other hand, a lean mixture will result in the motor's overheating, knocking and lack of power.

If unable to adjust carburetor satisfactorily, clean out all passages.

The passages may be cleaned by removing the passage plugs.

The carburetor air-cleaner, should be cleaned every 1000 miles. To clean, remove the outside cover. Filter unit (wire mesh) can then be slipped off leaving only air-cleaner back plate attached to carburetor. Wash filter unit thoroughly in a gasoline bath. When clean, allow to dry in the air for a moment or two. Then dip the unit into a very light solution of lubricating oil. Wipe off excess oil and reassemble.

TO REMOVE THE SIDE CAR WHEEL

Remove the inside fender brace bolts at the chassis. Remove the outside fender brace bolt at the axle. Loosen the clamps at the front of the fender. Then lift the fender up and forward. Remove 6 lugs around hub and slide wheel off spindle.

To remove the brake drum, take off the large inside axle nut. Take out the location bolt on the top axle housing. Drive the axle out of the housing. Slide the brake drum off.

To replace the brake drum bearing, remove the bearing nut lock screw located on the edge of the hub. Remove the bearing lock nut (part #37389) (left thread). Remove the felt washer and the felt washer retainer. Slide the bearing out of the hub.

TO RELINE REAR, FRONT AND SIDE CAR WHEEL BRAKES

Remove brake shoe springs. Lift shoes from brake plate. Punch out old rivets, remove old lining. New linings are drilled and counter sunk to accept new rivets on shoe. Assemble lining. Put in the two center brake lining rivets first, then proceed towards either end with rivets. Be sure to draw rivets well into lining to eliminate rivet heads bearing on drum.

TO REPLACE FRONT, REAR, AND SIDE CAR WHEEL BEARINGS

Remove wheel. Use screw driver to take out bearing lock screw on outside edge of hub. Remove bearing lock nut (left thread, part No. 37389). Remove felt washer and bearing thrust washer. Slide out hollow sleeve. Remove two retainers and the 24 rollers. Retainers are assembled in the hub with the closed ends back to back. Hardened steel ground bearing may be driven from hub if worn and replaced. Check rollers for wear, using micrometer. Standard rollers 1/4" .250. If rollers are worn .246, replace with new rollers. If the hollow sleeve bearing race shows wear or is flaked, replace.

When assembling, pack all bearings full of bearing grease. Be sure all felt washers and retainers are in place. Tighten bearing nut and lock screw.

SERVICING FRONT FORK

The front fork rocker arms must be well greased at all times to insure best operation. Rocker arm studs and bushings are hardened and ground. When these bearings wear and need replacing, jack up front of the machine until the wheel is off of the ground. Remove axle nut. Pull out axle. Remove the 6 studs holding wheel on brake drum. Disconnect brake arm. Disconnect brake cable at brake arm. Remove large nut on brake assembly and rocker arm. Remove brake drum and brake plate assembly from fork rocker.

Remove cotter pin. Drive out lower link end pins.

Remove rocker arm and fork end stud nut. Take assembly out of fork end.

Hold stud in vise. Remove center screw (right thread). Remove stud nut (left thread). Slide rocker arm off stud.

The hardened steel bushings may be pressed out of the rocker arms. New bushings replaced. If studs are worn, replace. Bearings must work free. Use Alemite Grease.

TO RELINE BRAKES OR REPLACE WHEEL BEARINGS
(See instructions under Side Car for relining all brakes.)

TO REMOVE THE SPRING FRAME ASSEMBLY FROM THE MOTORCYCLE
(refer to illustration 17A)

Remove the rear wheel and brake drum assembly.

Directly behind the top frame casting is a very small lock screw, counter-sunk into the frame casting itself. Remove this screw. This allows the uppermost chrome dust cover to be slid down out of the way.

Remove the one inch nuts (A) at the top and bottom of the spring assembly. Alemite fittings may be left in place.

Loosen the pinch bolt (B) on the lower frame casting.

From underneath the lower casting, unscrew the retaining cup (I).

Now get a piece of 2" hollow steel tubing with a 7/8" hole. Slide this tube up over the lower end of the shaft (F) that runs from the top to the bottom of the spring unit.

Using the nut (A) that you took off previously, screw this back on and tighten against the steel tubing placed on the shaft. This will draw shaft (F) down so that the complete assembly may be taken from the frame.

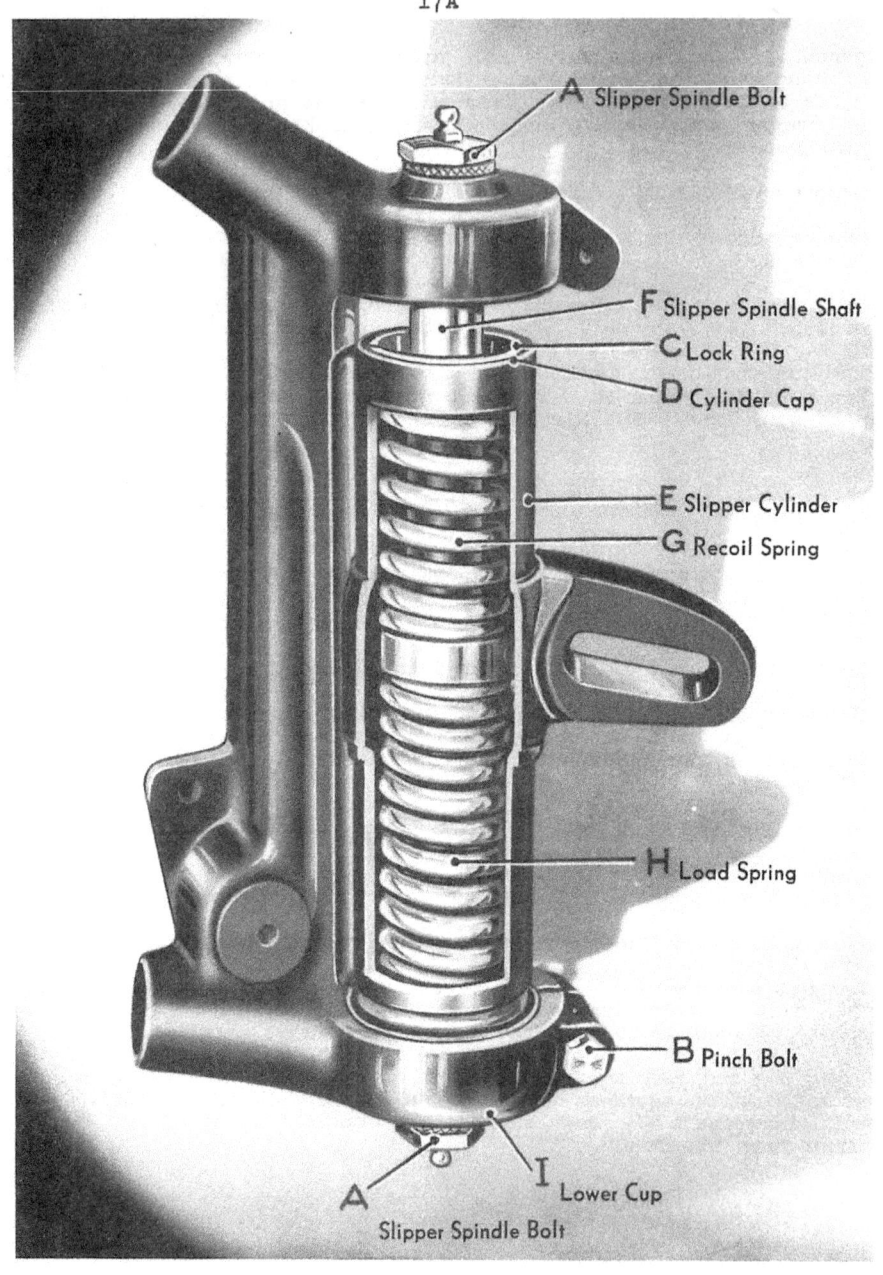

TO REMOVE THE SPRINGS FROM THE SLIPPER CYLINDER

The unit in which the spring action is housed (E) is referred to as the slipper cylinder. The shaft (F) is known as the slipper spindle. The nuts on top and bottom (A) are correctly known as slipper spindle bolts.

Remove the 2" piece of steel tubing that you used to compress the springs so that the unit could be removed from the machine.

Remove the lock ring (C) on the top end of the cylinder.

Compress the top spring (G) by placing the cylinder in an arbor press or large vice. This compresses spring (G) so that cap (D) may be unscrewed.

Remove cap (D) from the cylinder. The shaft and spring assembly may now be removed.

The top spring (G) is known as the recoil spring and is the shortest of the two. The bottom spring (H) is known as the load spring and is the longer of the two.

Spindle shaft (F) should work freely in the slipper cylinder bushings.

The taper end is the "top".

The 7/16 shoulder end of the shaft is the "bottom".

TO ASSEMBLE THE SPRING FRAME UNIT
(refer to illustration 17A)

Grease the springs.

Place the longest spring (H) with the large end toward the bottom into the slipper cylinder.

Take the slipper spindle shaft (F) and with the end with the 7/16 shoulder toward the bottom, slip it into the cylinder thru the spring.

Place the short spring (G) into the cylinder with the large end toward the "top".

Put cylinder cap (D) on the shaft. Place the entire unit in an arbor press or large vice and compress the springs in the cylinder so that cap (D) can be screwed into place. Screw cap (D) in until the slots in the cap line up with the cylinder casing (E).

Replace the lock ring.

Place the top chrome cover in position.

Compress the springs again by using the 2" piece of hollow tubing over the lower end of the shaft (F) and pulling it up with spindle bolt (A).

Slip the complete unit into the frame.

Slip the taper end of the spindle shaft (F) into the top frame casting and attach the top spindle bolt (A) with its grease fitting, just enough to hold it in place.

Remove the lower bolt (A) and take off the 2" piece of hollow tubing that you used to compress the springs.

Screw lower cup (I) into place, but do not tighten.

Now tighten the top spindle bolt (A).

Now take the lower cup (I) again and screw it up until you feel it strike. Then back off slightly and lock into position by tightening pinch bolt (B).

Screw the lower spindle bolt (A) into position.

Slide the chrome dust cover into place in the top frame casting and replace the small counter-sunk screw to lock it in place.

Keep the entire unit well greased during service with alemite grease.

TROUBLE SAVING TIPS

Don't race the motor on the stand. This abuse has ruined more motors than thousands of miles of road use.

Don't use inferior oils; use the oil recommended. It keeps the motor in good shape.

Don't neglect to oil all parts needed.

Don't fail to keep tires properly inflated at all times.

Don't spin the rear wheel when starting. Let the clutch in easily. Each time the wheel spins, rubber is torn from the tire, making it easier to puncture and reducing its mileage.

TROUBLE SAVING TIPS (Con't)

Don't open and close the throttle suddenly.

Try all nuts and bolts at least once a week. Any loose parts will be detected by regular inspection of this kind and will prevent trouble when operating on the road.

SOURCES OF MOTOR TROUBLE AND REMEDIES

1. Motor will not start.

    (a) - Gasoline supply exhausted, carburetor pipe shut off or clogged by dirt or water.

    (b) - Cylinder flooded by too much priming; pump out excess gas by kicking motor over just a few times with the throttle closed, and choke open.

    (c) - Mixture too lean. Adjust by directions.

    (d) - Oil congealed in motor; kick motor over a number of times before trying to start.

    (e) - Clutch slips, so that starter fails to turn motor fast enough. Tighten clutch.

    (f) - Distributor points dirty, pitted, worn out, or set too closely or too far apart.

    (g) - Compression very weak.

2. Motor stops continually after starting.

    (a) - Gasoline pipe clogged; motor will start on kicking but gets no more fuel. Disconnect pipe and clean.

3. Motor stopped suddenly.

    (a) - Gasoline tank empty, filler cap air vent plugged or gasoline pipe or carburetor clogged by dirt or water.

    (b) - Loose, broken or fouled spark plug or its cable unfastened.

    (c) - Oil supply in tank or engine exhausted; do not run until motor turns freely again; as severe damage to cylinder, piston or bearings will result; refill with oil and turn motor over slowly till chance of injury is removed.

4. Motor knocks.

   (a) - You are opening throttle too fast, or failing to retard the spark, when accelerating or in extremely hard pulling. Open throttle more slowly.

   (b) - Improper gas mixture, usually too lean. The correct mixture is a little hard to get; be patient and thorough; the result will greatly increase the motor's power and flexibility, and enable to pull hard hills without knocking, etc.

   (c) - Heavy carbon deposits; shows up on quick acceleration and when pulling hard hills; shows only when motor is hot.

   (d) - Overheated motor, due to low oil supply, or oil of poor quality. Sometimes due to running too fast in second or low gear.

   (e) - Distributor points set too far apart, making too early breaking of contact.

5. Motor shows lack of power.

   (a) - Overheated, due to heavy carbon deposit and other reason mentioned in paragraph under (Overheating".

   (b) - Faulty carburetor adjustment, usually too lean.

   (c) - Spark lever does not advance fully.

   (d) - Poor compression.

   (e) - Sump valve not working properly; clean screen and valve disc.

6. Motor overheats.

   (a) - Using poor grade of oil.

   (b) - Not using enough oil.

   (c) - Sump valve not working properly; clean screen and valve disc.

   (d) - Excessive carbon deposit.

   (e) - Weak valve springs; replace them.

(f) - Running with retarded spark.

(g) - Poorly adjusted carburetor.

(h) - Slipping clutch or dragging brake.

(i) - Running motor too fast in second or low gears.

(j) - Poor compression.

7. Motor misfires.

   (a) - Poor carburetor adjustment; usually too rich.

   (b) - Magneto or distributor faulty.

   (c) - Exhaust valve not seating properly; set too close.

   (d) - Spark plug points set wrong or in need of cleaning.

   (e) - Weak or broken valve springs; replace them.

   (f) - Sticking valve stems; usually exhaust, from poor oil, pour kerosene down valve stem till free.

8. Motor hard to start.

   (a) - Too much or too heavy oil in motor.

   (b) - Too much choking; clear motor of its excess gas.

   (c) - Weak kicking of the starter; give a sharp, powerful kick; it often takes a few days practice to acquire the knack of this.

   (d) - Poor carburetor adjustment; usually too lean.

   (e) - Spark plug points dirty or too far apart.

   (f) - Distributor points pitted, dirty, or too far apart, or too close.

9. Motor races when idle.

   (a) - Throttle does not close.

   (b) - Throttle cable not properly adjusted, or dry and needs oil poured down inside of cable casing.

   (c) - Worn throttle stem; replace.

OILING SYSTEM TIPS

Don't race motor while cold. Motor should be idled with spark advanced to warm up oiling system.

Check oil return pipe in oil tank. Note if oil is returning. After idling several minutes, oil fails to return, check oil line nuts and pipe, located under cam case from sump valve to pump, for leaks.

Check sump valve and crank case screws for tightness.

Oil filter may be filled with sediment. Test oil line from pump to oil filter. Remove line. Check oil flow.

Check crank case for high oil level by removing the top oil screw located on lower left side of crank case. Oil should never drain out thru this hole.

Should oil flow out this hole, it is a sure sign of too much oil in base, allowing the flywheels to dip in oil, causing over-oiling and possibly over-heated motor. The sump valve should be removed and cleaned. Check over valve seat for wear or sediment.

Clean sump valve parts and assemble. Be sure valve plate with valve and hole is assembled with this hole at lowest point of motor base.

The bottom screw on lower left side of motor base drains all oil from base. Drain motor base every change of oil in tank.

Flywheels should never spin in oil bath at bottom of crank case, with Indian dry sump lubrication.

The oil filter unit should be replaced every 10,000 miles.

LUBRICATION CHART
1940 Indian Seventy-Four, Model 340
(see illustration 25A)

1. CHAIN - See care and adjustment of chain.

2. REAR HUB - Pack with grease twice each season - see Care of Wheel Bearings.

3. SEAT POST - Grease every 200 miles.

4. GENERATOR - Few drops of light oil in oiler at each end of generator every 400 miles - see Care of Generator.

5. SADDLE FRONT CONNECTION BEARING - Grease every 200 miles.

6. GRIPS - Unscrew protector sleeve and inject a few drops of oil monthly.

7. HAND BRAKE LEVER AND CABLE - Oil hand brake lever pivot every 500 miles.

8. UPPER HEAD BEARINGS - Disassemble and pack with grease every season.

9. LOWER HEAD BEARINGS - Grease every 500 miles.

10. SPRING - Grease leaves when they squeak - see Care of Spring Fork.

11. SPRING END BEARING - Grease every 200 miles.

12. BRAKE ANCHOR LINK BEARINGS - Grease every 200 miles.

13. BELL CRANK END PINS - Grease every 200 miles.

14. BELL CRANK BEARINGS - Grease every 200 miles.

15. FRONT HUB - Grease every 1000 miles.

16. BRAKE CAM BEARING - Few drops of oil every 200 miles.

17. FRICTION WASHER - Keep free with a few drops of oil every 200 miles.

18. IMPORTANT - Keep drain hole clear to allow escape for excess lubricant in hub.

19. CONTROLS - Few drops of oil inside upper end of covering once a week.

21. BRAKE AND CLUTCH PEDAL - (Clutch pedal on left side) - Grease every 500 miles.

22. DISTRIBUTOR - Grease every 1500 miles.

23. SHIFT LEVER - Oil every 500 miles.

24. KICK STARTER SEGMENT BEARING - Grease every 500 miles.

25. BRAKE AND CLUTCH ROD CLEVIS - (Clutch rod on left side) - Few drops of oil on front and rear clevis pins every 200 miles.

26. SPRING FRAME - Grease every 1500 miles.

27. BRAKE CAM BEARING - Grease every 500 miles.

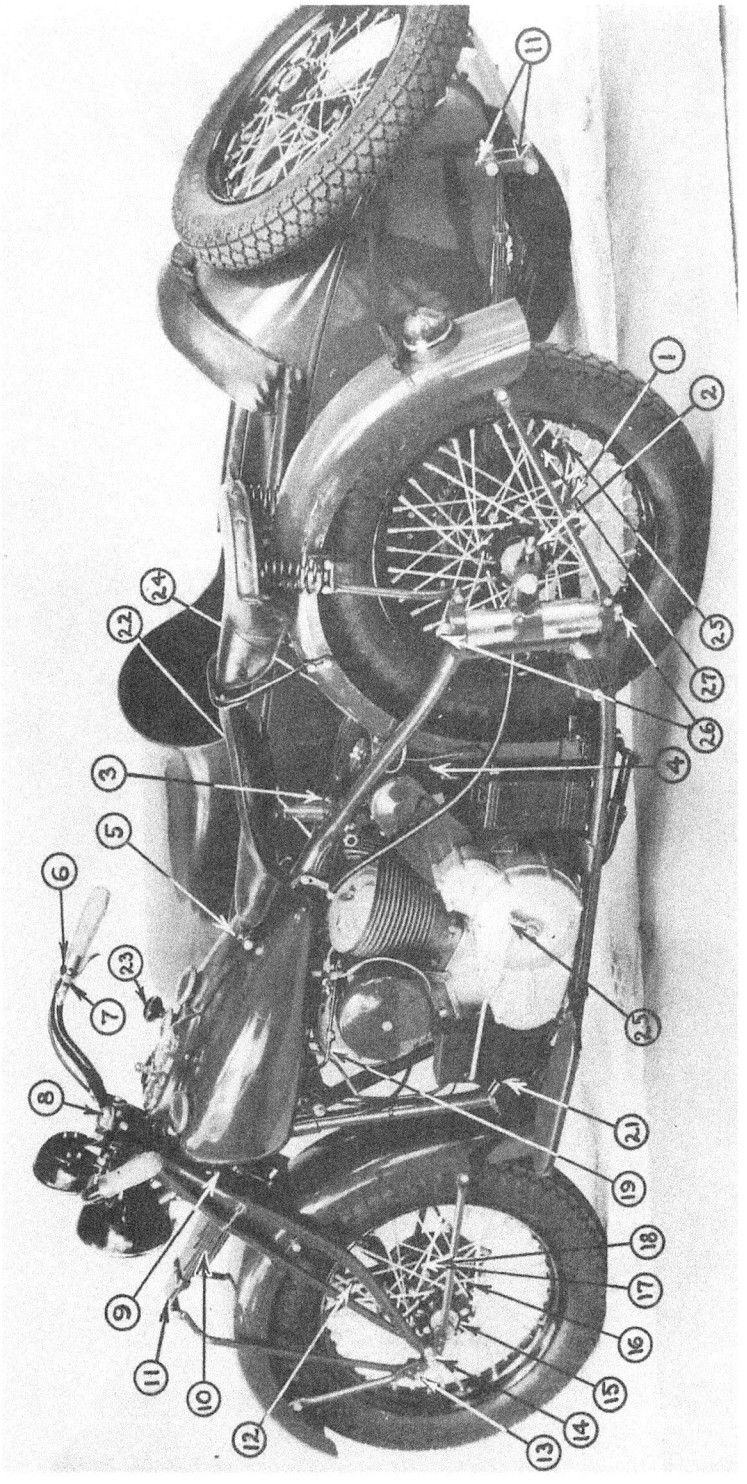

25A

©2013 Periscope Film LLC
All Rights Reserved
ISBN #978-1-940453-15-6

www.ingramcontent.com/pod-product-compliance
Lightning Source LLC
Chambersburg PA
CBHW070709050426
42451CB00008B/572